KAE TEMPEST is a poet. They are also a writer, a lyricist, a performer and a recording artist. They have published plays, poems, a novel, a book-length essay, released albums and toured extensively, selling out shows from Reykjavik to Rio de Janeiro. They received Mercury Music Prize nominations for both of the albums *Everybody Down* and *Let Them Eat Chaos*, and two Ivor Novello nominations for their song-writing on *The Book of Traps and Lessons*. They were named a Next Generation Poet in 2014, a once-in-a-decade accolade. They received the Ted Hughes Award for their long-form narrative poem *Brand New Ancients* and the Leone D'Argento at the Venice Teatro Biennale for their work as a playwright. Their books have been translated into eleven languages and published to critical acclaim around the world. They were born in London in 1985 where they still live. They hope to continue putting words together for a long time.

T0347687

ALSO BY KAE TEMPEST WITH PICADOR

Paradise

Running Upon the Wires

Let Them Eat Chaos

Hold Your Own

Brand New Ancients

ALSO BY KAE TEMPEST

The Line is a Curve

On Connection

The Book of Traps and Lessons

The Bricks that Built the Houses

Everybody Down

Hopelessly Devoted

Wasted

Everything Speaks in Its Own Way

Kae Tempest

Divisible by Itself and One

PICADOR

First published 2023 by Picador
an imprint of Pan Macmillan
6 Briset Street, London EC1M 5NR
EU representative: Macmillan Publishers Ireland Ltd, 1st Floor,
The Liffey Trust Centre, 117–126 Sheriff Street Upper, Dublin 1 D01 YC43
Associated companies throughout the world
www.panmacmillan.com

ISBN 978-1-5290-7311-9

Copyright © Kae Tempest 2023

The right of Kae Tempest to be identified as the
author of this work has been asserted by them in accordance
with the Copyright, Designs and Patents Act 1988.

All rights reserved. No part of this publication may be reproduced,
stored in a retrieval system, or transmitted, in any form, or by any means
(electronic, mechanical, photocopying, recording or otherwise)
without the prior written permission of the publisher.

Pan Macmillan does not have any control over, or any responsibility for,
any author or third-party websites referred to in or on this book.

3 5 7 9 8 6 4

A CIP catalogue record for this book is available from the British Library.

Printed and bound by TJ Books Ltd, Padstow, Cornwall

This book is sold subject to the condition that it shall not, by way of
trade or otherwise, be lent, hired out, or otherwise circulated without
the publisher's prior consent in any form of binding or cover other than
that in which it is published and without a similar condition including
this condition being imposed on the subsequent purchaser.

Visit **www.picador.com** to read more about all our books
and to buy them. You will also find features, author interviews and
news of any author events, and you can sign up for e-newsletters
so that you're always first to hear about our new releases.

it is beginning, just fingerings
At my knots,
Then will come rippings, and drenchings of
world-light

And my naked joy
Will be lifted out with shouts of joy –

And if that is the end of me
Let it be the end of me.

From *Orts* by TED HUGHES

ACKNOWLEDGEMENTS

These poems would never have seen the light of day
without the encouragement and support of Don Paterson;
thanks Don for lending me your ear this last decade. You've been
a great teacher to me. Thanks Colette Bryce and Rebecca Thomas.
And thanks to all the weirdos who make the world bearable.
My beautiful community. I love you so much.

Contents

Divisible by Itself and One

Sequence

Empty street beside the railway at night,
Spot-lit pigeons pecking at dropped bones,
Low houses lean in like a family
Portrait. Clapped-out van pulls up, the music
Playing loud. Drunken laughter from inside.
Woman clambers out with swollen suitcase
And goodbyes them all. She stops at her door
Looks up for a moon she can't see. Her eyes
Rank milk. The good times cling to her shoulders.
Long features, like a stretched mirror.
There, on the doorstep, she has the flooding
Sense that she is nothing but a sequence
Of events remembered differently by
Everyone involved. What she does not sense
Is the queue of silhouettes, stood behind,
Who pick up their right hands when she picks up
Her right hand and kick out their left legs when
She kicks out her left leg. When she calls out
To a great power she does not yet believe in
And asks to be opened, they raise their
Voices in solemn chorus behind her.

Body

The way she saw it, it was hers to hate.
Baggy jeans, shirts that came down to her knees
Or tops so short she couldn't stand up straight.

Grown-up voices crossed the street, *girl you'll freeze*.
Pale neighbours, their own lives being routine,
Swivelled when she passed, rattling their keys.

She liked it when it hurt. Liked playing mean.
She liked being where no one else would go.
She liked to not remember where she'd been.

At home later, she watched the water flow
And answered all their questions without words.
Some things are better picked before they grow.

She grabs fistfuls of belly fat. It hurts.
She wishes she could cut away her hips.
Instead, she goes to work, salutes the birds.

Pissing it down, her last cigarette rips.
Hot chocolate in a big cup, tiny sips.

*

Down by the cliffs, her woman in her lap.
All day for loving. Watching treetops float.
Light pushes through them. Sucking at the sap.

The chalk is damp. The cave a singing throat.
Scattered driftwood. Their faces bowls of light.
They ride each other's currents. Doze and gloat.

They crest the hill at last, their vision bright,
Their knees race the pedals the whole way down.
Reaching for each other. The tyres bite.

Sat around at dusk. Her body's her crown
Shining for the laughing friends beside her.
The fire kisses back. The sun goes down.

Whole crew chipping in for pills and cider.
Talk in abstract image, gently leaning,
Dancing till the outside is inside her

At last, no one else is intervening.
Her body is just sound. Without meaning.

Mountain road at midnight, Crete

I headed out into the night
jasmine on the wind.

The dark was like a losing fight.
It spat its tooth and grinned.

My solitude was lifted
by a gradual cigarette;

the more I try to fill the void
the bigger it will get.

I made my declaration on
the road between the pines,

everything was shaking as
I read between the lines.

The tablecloth, the coloured flags,
the aerial, the pit;

a thousand tiny clues that seem
apart, briefly lit.

The paving slab, the silent bell,
the bowl, the stick, the knife;

each separate thing a cell towards
the body of a life.

Everything is speaking
only some will comprehend

that all the murmuring and creaking
is of consequence to them.

I hold it to the light and see
the beauty in the fault.

All of it, alive. I find
the gate, draw back the bolt.

Up to my chest in heavy night
the jasmine like a spell.

Our lives are hung on solid things;
the washing line, the well.

The broken door, the leaning tree,
the step, the tap, the brick;

a living flame that domes around
a disappearing wick

Party, 4am

All your straight friends had kids
So you went out and made new friends
But the problem is
All your new friends *are* kids

Be careful that you don't become
a parody of yourself

state we're in what can we expect but hand-wringing on the one side and fist-throwing on the other work till there's nothing left of you but slouch on the sofa at the end of it all and shout no words at the empty room where no one lives but the things you settled for smoke till you pass out job done meanwhile the next generation are pulling their hoods up and all the bright hopes are singing I'm going to do things different ringing out across the rooftops like the call to prayer and you better do something because otherwise work till there's nothing left of you but slouch on the three-piece leather feet up on the glass coffee table and all the things that make it feel like it mattered it had to have mattered because otherwise what happened there used to be a river here flowing river and the houses round it we built our town out of what we would have done to keep the trouble out now the trouble's in we drink carbonated pineapple juice from aluminium cans and the flies are loud as motorbikes but nobody panic because there's a man at the helm whose hair is the same colour as his skin invoking the blitz spirit and nobody panic because technology wants us to live forever but only if you're beautiful and rich on the internet state we're in you're not getting any younger you better get up and get out there kiss your children eat your unfashionable meat shave your head and go get it what do you know of the thing that I carry through every damn day of my life this cess pit sucks the will to live a minute sober out of the strongest among us so don't talk to me about resilience or fortitude while you're peeking over my front garden to get a good look at the box my telly came in and how many cans was it this week clapping mosquitoes in my football shorts with my tits out saying I just want to make art good fucking luck I just want to connect with other human beings at least I'm trying you bunch of sour pigs

Getting on

I just woke up and it was here. Today
The furious ambition seems absurd.
How could it be I had so much to say?

I feel as jagged as the old blackbird
I spend the morning watching from the sink,
Awake since four, pecking at the wrong word.

Funny. My memory is on the blink.
My greatest wish is to be left alone.
I try and stay well back from what I think.

My main concern today; get the grass mown.
The changing light helps me manage the blues.
I feel as if my seams are all unsewn.

Let poems be the windows, not the views.
The stupid part was thinking I could choose.

*

I just got in, it's burning up out there.
The whole world interrupted by disease.
What had been solid ground gave way to air.

The feeling is when water starts to freeze.
The quiet of a change you can't deny,
The happening occurring by degrees.

Outside the sky is slow. The grass is high.
I sand the floors and barely speak two words.
Each motion for itself. No need to try.

It's not a case of wanting to be heard.
These days, it's more just hoping for the best.
Dog hair in white tufts, left for the bird.

It's all gone now, fur for her scratchy nest.
I walk the empty streets, hand on my chest.

*

I never really paid much mind to hope,
Long time since my pegs were all in tune.
I never was the type who couldn't cope.

Still, right above the house, the pointing moon,
Like it chose us, I sit on dusty bricks,
It's either here too long or gone too soon.

Your nails catch in my soles and my foot sticks.
I pull my leg, slow motion, from the trap.
The low stretch of your body turns and kicks.

Intent on new ground, dragging ancient scrap,
The path we find is one we've walked before.
We forge ahead, sure we'll disprove the map.

Let poems be the jug, not what you pour.
These days I dream of just enough. No more.

Flood

What scope is there for hope?
We wonder with our slogans worn like collars at the throat

Noah stood back from the boat
Drowning in the doubt that his own hands could make it float

Swear

And that's when god found themselves at pause beside eve's favourite sitting rock. The one they liked to climb before sunrise. The broad shelf of red stone was no different, as if it still expected them. And that pattern they'd been making with the woodpile, half-finished mandala they liked to watch from up high. Later, sitting heavily by adam's drawings, god's cavalier attitude was momentarily defeated by the animal portraits. Dabbing wistfully at a charcoal smudge which had never seemed that interesting before, god recalled the way adam had searched full days for trees opened by lightning so she could take her knife to the branches. Funny that gone feeling. That *give me space* feeling. Then – in the space looking around, too small for the room. And everything gone. Groaning in the empty garden in a moment that lasted till now, the almighty swore they'd never love again. And the words of the oath were famine, pestilence, genocide, flood.

Happy couple

It's true, of course, I served the tropes;
The milestones collapsed against.
Where *happy couple* meant cement
And *kisses*, desperate gropes.

And soon, neck-deep in solid core
I found myself with you, alone.
Sure things were going great at home
We kept our future there, in store.

We cast ourselves in words and deeds;
Things to do, tick off, attain.
What couples did. It seemed so plain.
I didn't know that I had needs.

Just did the simple things one does
Because they're done. That was enough.
I thought you complicated love
By always wanting to discuss.

The *whys* and *whats* were heavy loads.
I never could be natural. *Please
Just give me natural.* On my knees
To be the same as I supposed

The others were. *Just make me real.*
My shame became your burden then
I couldn't tell what was pretend
I wasn't there. I couldn't feel.

And in this state of push and pull,
Of high stakes wounds and buried stones
That smash the teeth when chewing down,
I wanted things routine and dull.

Just wanted to give like they gave;
Blindly, always. More than once
My words ran out, to snarls and grunts
The effort being far too grave.

What did it mean, this word *Commit*?
These disappearing lives? *Don't leave!*
Don't change or fall or want reprieve
Just stretch the mask and make it fit.

We quit the suffocating norm,
Our excavation; painful, long.
First one limb, the muscles gone
Then more, until we regained form.

Ran far enough to turn and say,
We made it out alive. We've seen
The whole lie burn. Let's build it clean
And do this thing for us, our way.

Even the youths shall faint and be weary

Isaiah 40:30

*I feel hope when I think about the next
generation.* Said us. The adults here.
Without so much as a satisfied burp.
Turps on a rag held to the nose. Nice buzz.
A box of painters snaffling at the oils.
Enjoying a well-earned pasta coma
while everything else spoils. Look. The Royals
breeding again. Lovely. Meanwhile, death
marks the face of the deep. Make a pile
of things to throw and things to keep. Tidy
till your bedroom feels like a place where
you can sleep. A shrine to you. Applaud it.

Watch us, sporting in the riptide. Tanning.
Maniac adults peddling hope. Surely
the kids will sort it. *So much more on it
than we were.* Terrible odds. Almost certain
they'll grow strong enough to restore truth.
Poor sods. No wonder they don't go outside.

Wind in the tall trees

pushing me
upwards   balancing
me from   beneath   and   smelling it keener
than spring in the rain I can feel it washing   me washing my hands
in its thin spring and washing my body it pushes   the sky
through   the trees   and the   trees move   like furious crowds
with a   purpose grown   taller than   each individual
purpose lost in a   moment of   union worth   nothing
less than the sum of all days   and
all nights and all   moments and also there's nothing
no human feeling   these are not   crowds or tall men with old faces
these are the product of sunlight and water mineral rich and
speaking in   patterns and   still it blows
through them floods the   high forest
with   movement
plays the whole
chorus like
chords
a new
shaking
power but
nothing
important is
happening
inconsequential
as wind last night the rain fell so hard
and so long I woke up without you and felt myself moving
through the walls and out there into the rain to be washed away
thrashed into mud and earth until the grass sprouted up from me in jagged bursts
that can't hide the baldness of mud or the hardness of stone and I lay there
returning while up in the treetops they bowed and they bowed

The actor dreams in character

House and a garden; toolbox, lawnmower.
Job that I leave at 5.00 every evening.

Mates in the pub on a Friday.
Fixing the motor outside at the weekend.

Kids skidding on knees at the wedding.
All these things I can't bear to want, I want.

Could have sworn I killed those dreams
but they got up and learned to hunt.

All be over soon.
Not much left hasn't turned,

gripped me and fucked me like I had no core.
Make me an actor who takes off the makeup

walks from the theatre, no less absorbed
than a passer-by. Let me end this performance

but surgery's real and my whole life's imagined.
The options are thinning,

the stakes are beginning to press down upon me
so how to stay balanced

and walk like the whole world is not out to punish
the parts of me I want to pleasure and kill?

Just give me a life let me husband and wife it
or at least, hold me tight till my shaking grows still.

Crush my grim mind back down into my body.
Slow my hurt brain up and make it go quiet.

Throw your big perfect shadow across me
and take me deep into the mouth of desire

where nothing's forbidden and nothing's required
and tell me I'll never be like them.

Us

Two fish on a plate
Open their eyes

Flight

Our

hands touch

on the steps

at the side of the stage.

The   sparks like   an   uprush

of birds taking   flight.

We connect.

Two routes converge

make a pathway.

The   beginnings of regrets   are   exciting

and direct.

I signal

I'm   about to take off

she signals she's prepared   to

keep pace.

It's time to change

direction. We lean into the rhythm.

Find   a   bar.

Pride

Pride by degrees. It's relative
I've carried my shame
like a drunk friend dragged
through the days of my life.
Damn dysphoria.

On a scale of *Can't-Bear-It* to *Pride*
I'm more proud than I was
but less proud than I'd like
of the beautiful thing
that we make when we make it.

Uncover a vast earth
inside a drawn breath,
sudden Eden.

But if your pride is hard
to get hold of. As fickle
as wind and so tight round
your shoulders you have
to dig deep to keep
motion, I love you. For
all your complexity.

All your sore edges.
All your torn corners.
All the long nights when you
poured forth, split the dull granite
to raw quartz. Sure as the
morning but floored by the
same old ache that came
crawling. No judgement. Just
movement. Keep walking
towards it. You're doing
it right. I'm all for you.

One hundred and eighty-three night stand

Six months since that night we met and now
I'm old enough to know if we could have it,
We wouldn't want it. Might have dragged the plough
Straight through each other and come out, ecstatic,
The other side. Surprised. Disentangled.
And managed not to speak again somehow

Reminder

Tides pull in pull out, I watch
Life is shorter than it was

I can't make myself behave
I do these fucking things because I did them

I face the blast
My face drops off, my skull is brass

Rains blow in blow out, I wait
Your advice is *Meditate*

You say: *Breathe in. Unclench your hands*
Your energy needs attention

Breathe out. Unfurrow your brow
Your energy lacks intention

My breath is molten glass
And nothing in this life will last

There is no beauty strong enough
To keep us from the hungry past

Who doesn't have a vice or four
To break the fall in times of stress?

Each day I bear you more and more
But can feel it less and less

Simple things

No matter how long we've been clucking for gold
Or bread
Or each other's bodies
Or each other's shoes
Or better brighter homes, futures, minds or television screens

All through the misery, sickness
The treachery
All through the want and the unrest

There was always the rain

There was always the wind through the rye in the evening
The silence of the deep night
The wide moon like a boat through tall buildings
And one lover alone on the road

There was always a pit in the earth for the bones
And a cloth on a hook in a kitchen
There was always a song being hummed by the water
Teenagers laughing at things only they understood

There was always a clean new morning, sober and fresh as the laundry
Coming up slowly
The prospect of *maybe today*

There was always the grace of a new resolution
Always the sound of the children sleeping
Slow breath as heavy as trust
And what you would do to protect them

There was always the key-change of friendship proven
Always the gestures older than words

Always the person leaving the ruins
Saying *this is my way, I must walk*

The impossibility of it

I used to write books
Now I write looks

Now I don't write
I just kiss and eat breakfast

Mountain

Sad as the wrong kind of weather, wet fleece
Getting sadder. Sad wind in the cold black
Night like an udder, pulling for release.

I throw rocks at the surface but it won't crack
Too cold for a new beginning. *Come back.*
Rain like nails. Car stalled for the slow geese.

They flock like cartoon aunties. Strut and flap
Towards the breathing mountain. We both wait
In our own ways for things to change. The tap

Won't turn off. I scrub till I break the plate.
I can't understand how it got so late
I was mid-scene when you started to clap.

Memories stand around outside. *No chance.*
There is no barn owl here no dappled horse,
There is no record playing, no slow dance.

Skinning carrots in pyjamas. The force
Of our nature is everywhere. Of course
It's your words I use when I speak to the plants.

You're too soft

Up at six. Prayers. Calisthenics. Make the bed.
I wilt for the strong man, the valiant head.
I want to be cared for and led. Tend to my needs.
Please. I want to be fed. I just want to be heard.
I want to have my words repeated back at me.
My thoughts exactly. Spread and re-spread.
I'm for the bold future. The glorious dead.
I'm for unbending will. Old-fashioned good sense.
Enough of your moaning now. I want your strength.
Stand up for something. Have principles.
Courage sustains me. I am what concerns me.
I am what I'm scared of. At last you have heard me.
Bright days ahead. Let's be sure of the journey.
We'll march back to nowhere in glorious step.

The loop

Fall asleep forgiven, wake up condemned.
Been stuck on the same loop since I was young
But even days like this come to an end.

Behave in ways that I can't comprehend.
Can't really say for sure whose will is done.
Fall asleep forgiven, wake up condemned.

Sometimes it feels more real to just pretend.
The past becomes the future. Leaves me numb.
But even days like this come to an end.

I walk the coast, the reeds rustle and bend;
Everything is moss and cautious sun.
Fall asleep forgiven, wake up condemned.

I tried to change for you. I tried to mend.
I broke the loop then found it re-begun
But even days like this come to an end.

Seems pointless climbing up, just to descend.
I climb. The repetition weighs a ton.
Fall asleep forgiven, wake up condemned,
Even days like this come to an end

These things I know part II

I know nothing

Best thing is to stick it out at all costs

Stronger not to push towards the exit
But stay here in the crush and try and breathe;
Strength is knowing when to bend, et cetera.
Root yourself and sway with every breeze.

That's what they tell me anyway, the beeches,
And for a time they seem completely right.
But how come none of them are slurring speeches
Or falling to their knees for some respite?

Sinking

Half-dressed, in the permanent
near nakedness of this love.
Called upon at any moment
to drop whatever's in
my hands. The pot,
the cup, the pen,
the toothpaste.
Morning rituals
broken by the
roaring of
our bodies
passing.
Your
moisture
like
a
bogged
field.
Startling
at
first.

Before

Megalithic long barrow

yeah yeah yeah yeah spinning
and everything spinning and when I need stillness I seek out the old stones.
Nothing but   sediment stacked up for centuries,
thousands of   years of unmoving,
mute as we all   should. Up on the mound
with the   old   stones watching the rain in the valley
but up here the rain   hasn't   reached us,
laid out on the rock   like a life in the sun
but it's grey as the   stone, tomb for a dead tribe
wild again, rooted   stone again, find me
whenever I'm slipping,   skipping slim stones
across a vast desert.   Drive myself
into the ground   for   some balance. Give
me one reason,   just   one
to stay standing or get out the   way let me
fall. I look up at   the trees,   staring into their faces,
light   through   the kiss of the leaves,
on the mound, on the cliff, in the river,   curled up in a cup made of old stone.

Fig

All night I lie awake with it, my want;
someone of my own I could flood with joy.
Each time I smell the sun inside a fig
or feel the suck of mud beneath bare feet,
I know the deep desire to belong.
God grant me completeness, so I can love.

I was told – watch out for those who need love;
unable to provide for their own want,
they'll seek out any partner, to belong.
They'll only put conditions on your joy,
smother your spirit, bind you at the feet;
they want you juiced as an overripe fig.

I reach up my hand towards the fig,
It comes so easily. I think of love;
how deeply I long to sit at their feet.
They ask me, full of pain, *What do you want?*
When I think of their face it's a song of joy,
increasingly, I can't make it belong.

At last, I had found my place to belong;
exacting an inspection of the fig.
The pinkness of its flesh, deep strands of joy;
an absolute image. The mouth of love.
If only we could have the things we want
instead of what will keep us on our feet.

I understand you better by your feet;
it's only in movement that they belong.
Hard-soled. Rhythmic. Heat-proof. They do not want,
just pass the days. As natural as the fig
that falls into the long grass of our love,
its heavy scent moans in the air like joy.

That summer, things changed, I bubbled with joy.
You took my shoes off to caress my feet.
Our tenderness was orchestral my love.
Come back to my embrace, where you belong.
Up there, right at the top, the last green fig
holds on; accept what is and do not want.

I do not want to suffocate your joy,
just curl up in the feet of that great fig,
feel your breath rising and belong to love.

Do it for the joy

The line in the sand is a chalk outline.
A furious loathing had sprung up between
factions, and people spent their days sneering
at each other's deeply held beliefs. The scenes
passed in explosions. Our panic roared back
like hills. We told ourselves this talk of emergency
was an elitist ploy. Or the hysterical madness
of a doomsday cult led by a teenage child.

A teenage child gazed out of the kitchen window,
studied the two pigeons that had alighted
on next door's roof, and felt the ancient pause.
Plucked from their chores by the birds at rest.
Their washcloth submerged in thick water until
the birds fell upwards to flight. Chasing
the air through the chimney stacks. Relics
of a different London. Strange as our own.

Cocoon

Thank god on the floor on my face on the concrete thanking the beautiful deep down current in the earth for all the pain in my soul and the freak in my body because it means I am living, I am growing. It comes back to me again about the caterpillar, I'm sure you've heard it said by sober friends in earnest tones, how even after their hairy little magnificent body has gone through all that pain, that pulsing, that glorious metamorphosis, they still have to fight their way out of the fucking cocoon and so fuck it they fight and they fight and they fight and even though loads of them die from exhaustion some make it out, some do and those that do make it out, those that break through the walls into the light, that do persevere through the pain of that binding, only then, after all that fight, will they have developed the muscles they need to spread those new wings, out there in the world. Without that fight they can't build enough strength to fly once they're out, and they would just die pretty much the very minute they got to the light. So, every single time you see one remember how hard she had to push ok? Remember how hard he fought to fly past you pretty as summertime minding his business

Absurd

No matter who you end up with you'll end up in absurdity. Them, naked at a bowl of hot water infused with thyme, an apron over their head for their sinuses. You, leant heavily against the back door, staring out. It starts with friends round and dog walks and dancing but it all strips away to them naked, a fuzzy shape through tired eyes, your smeared glasses in your hand so you can cry better. Their small shaved head a peanut of raw confusion as they prompt you using internet words you don't understand, until at last, you admit that everything you suffer is your own fault and there's a part of you that will die this death with anyone so why not die it with this one? Why not stick it out with this insane human being, rather than dig it all up just to replant yourself in a parallel hole.

As useless a memory as any other

The first night in the stone house
in the foothills
you had a bad dream.

I woke to your movement
and noticed the black
of the shuttered stone bedroom.

That first morning
you woke before me and opened the shutters
and I felt you climb back into bed.

We watched the sun lick through the leaves
and up over the hills
as the mist smoked up from the grass.

Alright
you said
I will marry you.

I place this moment
in a frame I have carved
from the wood of alone beneath a wet grey sky

tough clouds cuss
the pavements of Lewisham
and I have so much to learn

of what a person can and can't bear.
We hold till our arms ache from holding.

Brother

I was in the pit. But instead of taking myself by the arm and guiding myself up the wet sides, one impossible handful of mud at a time, I just lay there in it. Dead. Unable to turn off the TV in case my brain. And eventually when I had managed to not be drunk for long enough I did find myself able to drag my huge and aching legs up the stairs and put myself to bed where I lay on my face and kept the light on. I forgot I had friends I could have called. I forgot about you, my brother. With your wide open face and your deep wrinkles and your thin strong body that smells of high grade and your kind coughing smile and your baggy clothes, leaning back in your chair with your legs crossed at the ankles and your beats playing through glitchy speakers wired in complicated ways and your glasses with one arm falling off from where your daughter pulled them apart and your tangled beard and your slow chewing mouth and your eyes half closed, gelled from the daily blaze. I forgot I could have just walked the grey miles to your studio and put myself in the hands of our childhood again and said brother I'm low and felt your deep wisdom your wild anger your safe brown hands clutching my shoulder saying *punches in bunches* or something like that.

Choices

How good are you at not doing it when
you tell yourself not to? Really? How hard
do you find it to drag yourself back from
the edge of the precipice? My lord,
it's so much easier to know what's best
than to do what's best. I mean. Feel that pull.
A thousand tiny strongmen in my chest
stretching the rope and expecting the fall.
One day, I'll want the things that wound me less.
Yes. Let it soothe me. Make dull noises.
Indulge in slow motion montages.
Grand concepts. Myself in mint condition.
When actually, it's in the small choices.
It's in the decision. Or the indecision

Crush

I feel you like a threat.
Like some danger on the move
that hasn't happened yet.

I feel you like a change.
Like something coming on
that hasn't had to age.

I want you like an end.
Like when I'm at my weakest
and I cannot comprehend.

I leave. I drive for hours.
Until the trees surrender to the cliff
the wave devours.

I sleep out in my car,
the weather like a trashy film,
and wonder where you are.

I try to clear my head
but behind every door
I find the hunger to be led,

your face in silhouette.
The wind against the breaking wave,
I feel you like a threat.

The more you know the less you know :‖

We gain our fragile station
From our labour. But the wage

Of a lifetime's education
Is the blankness of the page

New world order online at your convenience

Most likely, there is no way back from this.
Good sleepers find themselves awake at night.
Lying half on, half off the precipice.

Simple interactions are fight or flight
As if rules apply or even exist.
We all know what's gone on. Nice to be right.

Here's to it. Nothing is clear but the mist.
Tagging our kinks in our profiles. Awed
By the dullness of life in the abyss.

We are a collective farce. Just reward
For our suffering. Describing a meme
We saw by chance. Scrolled past when we were bored.

Remembering posts like things from a dream.
Intrusive opinions. Constant impact.
So absorbing, to gaze into the stream.

Direct to skull from tablet. *I THINK THAT
IT WAS ALL FORETOLD.* Don't forget to send.
The vaccine's not a satanic contract.

The mark of the beast that signals the end
Will not be implanted into your wrist.
It's in your pocket already, my friend.

Morning

I press my ear against the phone to hear your lips
part and re-part. Your skin is the coming day,
your eyes last night's embers. You like it when
I stop your mouth against the wall. Morning
blasts of giddy sunlight through your curling hair.
Your cheeks flushed with moaning and the shower
slamming down, saying *life's a chance to do*.
It's all been done before. We make it new

Amie

Early beauty. Heavy sun. Dark water.
Glad as clouds. The green smell of coming rain.
Talking softly with me at the counter,
Fingers at my temples. The pounding train
Above our heads, pushes its electric
Across our bridge. We lean into the grain.
I map planets in your freckles. Our kiss
Is vaster than its edges can contain.

Mountain beauty. As full as the river.
Old as London. Slow as moving light.
Old as every dream drowned in that water.
Walk me across the bridge into the night.
Show me my city like I've never seen it.
You make me someone I have longed to be:
Spinning round this dirty town I feel it
Open its dirty mouth and smile at me.

I want to sing you early songs. Go deeper.
I want to take you back where you began,
Find the scraps of you you hid in secret
And bring them back to life beneath my tongue.
I stood before you in the rain that day,
The Thames a rolling dice, a careful word.
The sudden downpour came as if to say
No matter what we did, it would be heard.

Give and take

He went back to nurse the brute. For love.
He saw it like – at least it can't get worse
than what it was. And so he packed his stuff.

No horse and cart. No wreaths lining the hearse.
Just a wooden box and a can of stout.
Kept searching his hands like an empty purse.

She died as she lived. A nightmare. Devout.
Quick to tell him he was going to hell.
He used to blame her. Now he has no doubt

that blame and anger make a person swell.
Swore to himself, as her body broke down,
he would not live that poison, but be well.

He holds on, despite what would have him drown.
Overwhelmed but still, he gets through the day.
It *does* go on. He keeps her dressing gown.

Feels cold to miss a person that he hated
for so long. She comes back to him, all grey
in his dreams. Rotting. Disintegrated.

She begged for an end to it. Grim display.
The soul trapped in mutinous flesh. What if
he could up the dose, get out of the way?

You drink, you shout, you clean, you ache, you live.
As much as it is possible to give.

*

Life is a transaction, she said. What's fair?
Nothing. If she wanted it she chored it
and what she couldn't steal she got elsewhere.

Fresh starts are for those who can afford it,
otherwise it's the little things. Make do
with watching out the window. Who caught it

off of who and how it's getting round. Grew
tired of him on about what had gone wrong.
No patience for all that, she told him too.

If you can put up with it, life is long.
The more that you've borne, the more you can bear.
That's how a person learns if they are strong.

He cut her off. He stopped. He left her there.
She didn't turn her back on him. He said,
can't be around you. Don't mean I don't care.

Bless him, she thought. He doesn't see the thread
he carries through his life leads back to her.
He can't just wish the brain out of his head.

She often sensed his outline though, dark blur
moving behind her, as slow as a lake.
She'd clean her glasses, stir the tea. Re-stir.

The rain, the pipes, the long nights spent awake.
As much as it is possible to take.

Love song for queens, studs, butches, daddies, fags and all the other angels

Ever felt wrong. Like so wrong, like please just cut my body off
and never look at me in fact don't touch me. I like you it's not
that.

It's these hips this chest these things on me, they aren't mine and
they make me flinch when you touch me. I don't. It's not that
I don't like, but please you can't understand.

I want to kill it. All these parts. And the things that I can't be are
bad they are a wound and I can't. But what she heard was none
of this just silence.

My head turned away from hers and I could feel her *is it me? am I
not doing* but had no language then or ever, could not speak the
real words.

All I had was what I didn't have and couldn't be. I never even
knew the words and plus each time laughed at looked at moved
away from in the party.

All that shame and dirt inside that makes you even harder. But
she was always good to that part. That part of me that was, that
wasn't.

That couldn't breathe without her there to touch and make and
how is it for you to have been underneath their sickness your
whole life?

Their sickness that says girls and boys and sir and miss and also
hers and his and every other violent word that means not you,
you're not, you can't. Yeah smile for them.

Straighten up do what you can if you can, fluff your hair or
    different clothes or smile that's fine I can't. I used to though
I never could. I tried. I really tried. I'm sorry that I wasn't there
    for you. I was ashamed of me. I was ashamed of the you in me
    that people saw
when they saw dyke and sin and wrong. And all the ugly things
    they saw.

I just wanted to be on the winning team. I liked the feeling of
    walking with strong men. Straight and boring and small in
    their ambitions and mean to other people.
I laughed along. I almost liked it. I see it now. They were not
    strong. As if.
But you? You are the strongest ones among us. Daring as you do to
    live. Wholly as you are. While the rest of us go straight

to pieces for what we can't bear to admit we carry. The whole grim
    world restrained or restraining. Pretending the void has not
    unfurled
has not hurled them down. Does not contain them. I hear you
    whisper *honey don't run from desire so long it'll turn you to stone.*
You'll only end up angry and breaking whatever you can. Please. Put
    your arm around me, you stunning human, all made up
with that strong chest those eyes like prayers, kiss me and tell me
    it's not too late. Call me handsome call me boy, because you see
    it. I don't have to say.

I didn't know back then how to walk with you. You were too
     beautiful for me. Too bold. Your colour was so bright I faded
     out, even though, thank god
I knew at last I'd seen myself and found my people, my own
     siblings. There was still so much in me too locked up to dance.
The truth is ugly. I was scared I wasn't like you either.

I had it all inside, I strapped it on and fucked in secret. Trust me
     I know what it is to be alive, but I smothered it in normal.
     Threw myself into my work.
Nice quiet life.
This solemn effort expended. Unending pretence.
For the approval of people that despise us.
To abide by rules that hurt us.
To achieve a happiness that will kill us.

But every time I got high as in pushed myself up to the limit of
     high, like no way back that kind like
losing language, losing motor neurone coordination like after up
     three nights for what, for no way back for acid in the morning.
Then the next night, was it day, there it was always the same,
     regular as trains. Out to play. My deep deep want my deep
     deep train of want and I went down
straight under, crushed by it, the heavy heavy beauty of my need
     for you who I turned my back on, for you who I tried so hard
     to not resemble. For You.

My people. My beautiful people. My beautiful trans people,
  natural as life.
I'm so sorry I was not in your love sooner.
I have been so cold without you. I wish I'd spent all these years in
  your arms and close to you
and had you shave my head and slap my back and take me under
  your soft wing and fight with me each time I had to fight and
  teach me things I had to learn alone.

And when you hear this, you know who you are, accept me please
  accept my love.
I love you. I am here.
It might feel like I'm far away, not with you right up close because
  the stage the screen the page.
I am.
I'm right beside you.